Arranged by Bill Galliford
and Ethan Neuburg

udio recordings produced by
Dan Warner, Doug Emery,
and Lee Levin

POP & COUNTRY
INSTRUMENTAL SOLOS

CONTENTS

All Rights Reserved. Printed in USA.

ISBN-10: 1-4706-4093-7 (Book & CD)
ISBN-13: 978-1-4706-4093-4 (Book & CD)

SHAPE OF YOU

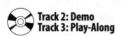
Track 2: Demo
Track 3: Play-Along

Words and Music by
KEVIN BRIGGS, KANDI BURRUSS,
TAMEKA COTTLE, ED SHEERAN,
JOHNNY McDAID and STEVE MAC

Shape of You - 2 - 1

Track 4: Demo
Track 5: Play-Along

FEEL IT STILL

Words and Music by
JOHN GOURLEY, ZACH CAROTHERS,
JASON SECHRIST, ERIC HOWK, KYLE O'QUIN,
JOHN HILL, ASA TACCONE, ROBERT BATEMAN,
GEORGIA DOBBINS, WILLIAM GARRETT,
FREDDIE GORMAN and BRIAN HOLLAND

Feel It Still - 2 - 1

HOW LONG

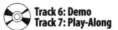

Track 6: Demo
Track 7: Play-Along

Words and Music by
CHARLIE PUTH, JUSTIN FRANKS
and JACOB HINDLIN

Moderate rock (♩ = 110)

How Long - 2 - 1

THERE'S NOTHING HOLDIN' ME BACK

Track 8: Demo
Track 9: Play-Along

Words and Music by
SCOTT FRIEDMAN, SHAWN MENDES, TEDDY GEIGER
and GEOFFREY ELLIOT WARBURTON

There's Nothing Holdin' Me Back - 2 - 1

ATTENTION

Words and Music by
CHARLIE PUTH and
JACOB KASHIR HINDLIN

Attention - 2 - 1

SAY SOMETHING

Words and Music by
CHRIS STAPLETON, MOWF DANJA,
LARRANCE DOPSON, TIMBALAND
and JUSTIN TIMBERLAKE

Say Something - 2 - 1

Track 14: Demo
Track 15: Play-Along

BELIEVER

Words and Music by
ZACHARY BARNETT, JAMES ADAM SHELLEY,
MATTHEW SANCHEZ, DAVID RUBLIN,
SHEP GOODMAN and AARON ACCETTA

Believer - 2 - 1

Believer - 2 - 2

Track 16: Demo
Track 17: Play-Along

MEANT TO BE

Words and Music by
JOSH MILLER, TYLER HUBBARD,
DAVID GARCIA and BEBE REXHA

Meant to Be - 2 - 1

Track 18: Demo
Track 19: Play-Along

ONE FOOT

Words and Music by
BEN BERGER, RYAN MCMAHON,
RYAN RABIN, ELI MAIMAN,
NICHOLAS PETRICCA, KEVIN RAY
and SEAN WAUGAMAN

One Foot - 2 - 1

Track 20: Demo
Track 21: Play-Along

HAVANA

Words and Music by
BRIAN LEE, LOUIS BELL,
CAMILA CABELLO, FRANK DUKES,
BRITTANY HAZZARD, ALI TAMPOSI,
ANDREW WATT, YOUNG THUG
and PHARRELL WILLIAMS

Moderate latin rock (♩ = 104)

Havana - 2 - 1

THE CHAMPION

Track 22: Demo
Track 23: Play-Along

Words and Music by
CARRIE UNDERWOOD, BRETT JAMES,
CHRISTOPHER BRIDGES and CHRIS DESTEFANO

BROKEN HALOS

Words and Music by
CHRIS STAPLETON and MIKE HENDERSON

Track 24: Demo
Track 25: Play-Along

PARTS OF A TRUMPET AND FINGERING CHART

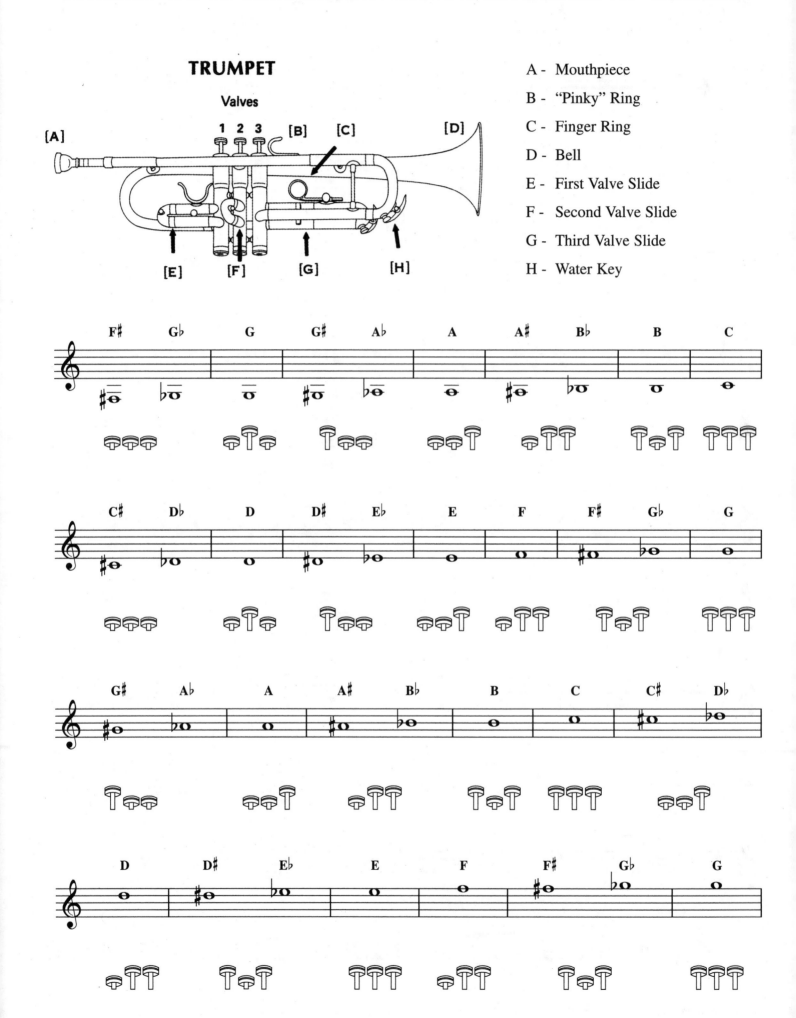